Sailing to Babylon

Sailing to Babylon

POEMS BY

James Pollock

ABLE MUSE PRESS

Able Muse Press

www.ablemusepress.com

Printed in the United States of America

Library of Congress Control Number: 2011940157

ISBN 978-0-9865338-7-7

Foreword copyright ©2012 by Jeffery Donaldson

Cover images:

   - *Sailing Ships from Heaven* by Roger-Michael Goerge
   - *Ye Olde Stock - Compass* by Pau Norontaus

Cover & book design by Alexander Pepple

Able Muse Press is an imprint of *Able Muse:* A Review of Poetry, Prose & Art—at www.ablemuse.com

Able Muse Press
467 Saratoga Avenue #602
San Jose, CA 95129

for my mother
Irene Pollock, née Helberg

and in memory of my father
Philip Pollock (1924-2001)

Acknowledgments

I am grateful to the editors of the following journals where many of these poems originally appeared, often in different versions:

AGNI: "Northrop Frye at Bowles Lunch," "Glenn Gould on the Telephone"

The Dalhousie Review: "The Poet at Seven"

The Del Sol Review: "Prague"

The Fiddlehead: "Grandmother's Bible," "House," "Prow," "The Museum of Death"

Geist: "Northwest Passage" (Henry Hudson, his final voyage 1610-11)

Grain Magazine: "Map of the Interior"

Maisonneuve: "Radio"

The Nashwaak Review: "*Ex Patria*" (as "Houston"), "Mortgage"

The Paris Review: "Northwest Passage" (as "Northwest Passage: After Cavafy")

Riddle Fence: "A Weekend in Vienna"

Southern Poetry Review: "Sailing to Babylon"

Thanks to editors Don Selby and Diane Boller for selecting "Northrop Frye at Bowles Lunch" for republication in *Poetry Daily*, and to editors Lorna Crozier and Molly Peacock for listing "The Museum of Death" in *Best Canadian Poetry 2010*.

Many thanks to Loras College for several travel awards, a reassigned time award, and a sabbatical, all of which were indispensable in writing these poems. I am grateful to the Bread Loaf Writers' Conference at Middlebury College for a waiter scholarship, and to Western Michigan University's Prague Summer Program at Charles University for a John Woods Scholarship in poetry. Much gratitude to Inprint, the University of Houston, and the University of Houston Creative Writing Program for an Inprint Dissertation Fellowship, a C. Glenn Cambor/Inprint Fellowship, a Stella Ehrhart Memorial Fellowship, and a Cullen Educational Trust Graduate Fellowship, all of which provided crucial early support. Many thanks as well to York University for a John S. Proctor Entrance Scholarship, which enabled me to begin my apprenticeship in the art.

For their criticism and encouragement in the writing and revision of these poems, I am grateful to Andrew Auge, David Baker, Michael Collier, Jeffery Donaldson, Mark Doty, Linda Gregerson, Seamus Heaney (for a memorable conversation), Edward Hirsch, Joan Houlihan, Richard Howard, Jeffrey Levine, Philip Levine, Rosanna Warren, and Adam Zagajewski. Particular thanks to Carmine Starnino, and to my editor, Alexander Pepple.

I am very grateful to my parents, my brother, and my sisters for their support and encouragement over many years, and to my son Felix for sharing me with this book. And thanks beyond words to my wife and in-house editor, Stormy Stipe, for her sharp eye and ear, and especially her love and support.

Wandering where home is . . .

I sailed a boat to Babylon
and rowed back lonely in the rain.

The foreword. It is the art of setting a table without using any cutlery. There is so much silverware in James Pollock's first book that I would like to take up from its measured place . . . admire its polish, consider my reflection in. But to be overly particular at this stage about "what goes with what" would be to distract from the excellent feast that lies before you. I would almost prefer to be the reviewer, or some boastful exegete revealing to readers one hundred years from now some of the untold treasures that, its many readers notwithstanding, lie hidden here still.

It isn't often a compliment to say of a book that, reading it, you don't know whether you are coming or going. It takes a poet of Pollock's lyric gift and intellectual maturity to make it so. We are coming *and* going. Our explorations (poetic, spiritual, familial, cultural) are most *at home* in ironies of just this sort, that is, when we trade in our usual *either/or* dialectics for a more inviting, but also more challenging, *both/and* configuration. Poems can be about exploration of course, if they like, but at a deeper level they are embodied explorations themselves, explorations into the unknown, explorations in exile. The poem, we feel in our age of chronic slippage and self-effacement, is *far from itself,* exiled from such conditions as were long ago spoken for, and too often now spoken against. Since it is in their nature, as in ours, the poems we make go in search of them still, among their own ruins, as it were.

Pollock does not shy from naming the central archetypes of his book or from putting them in the front windows of his poems (always the sign, I've felt, of a writer who has his bearings, knows where he is). He is the map maker, finding new ways into our unexplored "interiors" ("Map of the Interior"). He is the archeologist, unearthing buried artefacts, whose meanings, taken for what they are, may yet awaken an urgency in our searches ("Prow"). He is the Dantean wanderer-in-mid-life looking for the way upward and on. The guide, the bird-like harbinger, the opened and the inherited book, the *abiding* house, the quasi-Sisyphean climb to imagined heights and their prospective views: these make up part of the book's symbolic inventory, images that appear to search among one another for that unique orientation that will show the poetry's way both out into experience and back into itself.

With its quiet double-take, the title of the book recalls us not only to the biblical conditions of Babylonian exile, of a people displaced from its own roots, but to W.B. Yeats's "Sailing to Byzantium" and its own inveterate searches. Yeats's Byzantium is in more ways than one an imaginary place, whose reality and expression are largely the mappings-out themselves of artistic endeavour. The domain of art—with its would-be monuments of unaging intellect—is where "old men" would be most at home, he implies, most *not in exile* from where they belong. Yeats himself came to revise this notion of absolute arrival in his subsequent poem "Byzantium," where the sense of a necessarily continuous *agon* is magnified and built back into ideas of the finished and the monumental. This is Pollock's correction as well, though he goes further still, with an eye to ironizing our own ironic axioms. Today, we seem more than ready to think of ourselves as permanently *in exile.* We pridefully renounce our Odyssean nostalgias, which at their root were not nostalgic at all in the way we normally think of it. They were not merely a search for the *nostos* (as though roots themselves were always heading for home), but a search in relation to it, around and about, over and against. Its bearings, however far from them we may wander, provide us with a continuous orientation. The danger of being indifferently *not at home,* Pollock advises, is the danger of being exiled from the meaning of exploration.

Such resources made available to a border-crossing expat-Canadian like Pollock are sweet indeed. The heroic and also failing search for the Northwest Passage through an inhospitable environment is one of the abiding myths of the Canadian imagination, and Pollock is intuitively at home in it. That is, to have been born there is to have been born *in* the land of mythically doomed expedition. It means not having to leave home to go exploring there. His homage to Glenn Gould is, whatever else, an homage to this very spirit. Pollock then, a haunted *voyageur* by instinct and birthright, *goes away* in this book to travel and explore the world, and in so doing effectively throws his northwest passage into reverse. It becomes the origin from which he departs. In her poem "Questions of Travel," fellow expat Elizabeth Bishop asks the question that abides at the heart of *Sailing to Babylon:* "Should we have stayed at home, wherever that may be?" Heading out to *go looking*—to live elsewhere in every sense—is, on Pollock's map, to exile oneself from the original conditions of exploration, and therefore to go in search of them again.

How then do we find our way back to *the place we had in mind* when we first went looking for the way back? One answer is, "You can't." Another is, "Go ahead and try, knock yourself out." One finds such responses in one's travels. A subtler answer, and a reversing irony, would be to search among the fellow searchers, try to find your way back to *them*, or at least to something still available in their expeditions. Their echoes—beholden to no national boundaries—abound. Look for Dante wandering in the centerpiece of this book, "Quarry Park," where the poet follows his child guide into and through a remembrance of things past. He is masterfully embodied in the poem's ascent motif and in Pollock's own (in every sense!) unerring terza rima, in whose alternating ingress and egress the poet finds momentary stays on the way to the marvelous *Paradiso* at its close. Robert Frost's own journeying in "The Woodpile" wanders ghostily in this same poem (replete with a know-nothing, know-it-all bird who leads the way), with its accompanying search for the "ruins that prevail" that prevail in these echoic ruins. Keats's "On First Looking into Chapman's Homer" whispers to us within "The Poet at Seven." Something of Amy Clampitt's ornithological imagination flitters throughout. And we don't forget Yeats.

It is part of this poetry's *both/and* orientation, that its searching among its own ruins for the authority of further exploration should become in part the form of further exploration it seeks.

At last I take a volume,
open its paper cover
like a hatch, and my mind climbs down

to the half-remembered
country I have left.

You will hear in these poems something like the jouncing and ruckus of a wilderness traveler adjusting the gear on his back, steeling his resolve, finding his footings and heading off. But for where? In the end Pollock's departures are an exploration of that inward Northwest Passage where the borderlines themselves between real and imagined, the present and the past, the found and the lost, seem almost to dissolve—passages, as Pollock says, "breaking up within"—and where, in this anthem of mixed voices, our wondering where home is becomes our wandering where home is.

—Jeffery Donaldson

CONTENTS

Sailing to Babylon

Northwest Passage

after Cavafy

The Franklin Expedition, 1845-48

When you set out to find your Northwest Passage
and cross to an empty region of the map

with a headlong desire to know what lies beyond,
sailing the thundering ice-fields on the ocean,

feeling her power move you from below;
when all summer the sun's hypnotic eye

won't blink, and the season slowly passes, an endless
dream in which you're forever diving into pools,

fame's image forever rising up to meet you;
when the fall comes, at last, triumphantly,

and you enter Victoria's narrow frozen Strait,
and your *Terror* and *Erebus* freeze in the crushing floes;

in that long winter night among the steeples
of jagged ice, and the infinite, empty plain of wind and snow,

when the sea refuses to be reborn in spring,
three winters pass without a thaw, and the men,

far from their wives and children, far from God,
are murdering one another over cards;

when blue gums, colic, paralysis of the wrists
come creeping indiscriminately among you;

and you leave the ships, and set out on the ice,
dragging the lifeboats behind, loaded

with mirrors and soap, slippers and clocks,
into the starlit body of the night,

with your terrible desire to know what lies beyond;
then, half-mad, snow-blind, even then,

before you kill the ones who've drawn the fatal lots,
and take your ghastly communion in the snow,

may you stumble at last upon some band of Inuit
hauling their catch of seal across the ice,

and see how foolish you have been:
forcing your way by will across a land

that can't be forced, but must be understood,
toward a passage just now breaking up within.

I

Radio

The kitchen dark, the summer night air warm,
and my father at the kitchen table, radio

turned down low, alone, listening to baseball.
My mother and I come inside from our swim,

toweling off. The crowd is restless. Long silences
between pitches in the play-by-play.

Look how he holds the radio in both hands
like a steering wheel, thumb on the tuning dial

to catch the wavering channel, fighting static.
His eyes glitter like a field of fireflies.

The Poet at Seven

If only he could watch his teacher read
and, gazing, could lean there at his desk
in the winter light of Hillcrest Public School
and listen as she speaks the strangest words—
with her vivid face, her braided hair
and dark eyes like a real and ordinary
siren's—if only he could wait like that
forever while Miss Harmon reads *The Odyssey*
(his kind young teacher with the ringing voice
he loves so much he lets the story sing
into his heart), she would peal out for him,
swaying above him like a slender bell,
the breaking changes of a life to come.

My Grandmother's Bible

Mary Pollock, née McConnell (1887-1959)

The shape, the heft, of a shovelful of sod.
A sheaf of God. Its soft-worn pebbled grain

of supple Levant morocco. Two rips
yawn along the spine two inches long,

a strip of leather's lacking at the top.
The pages, inked in foxed and well-thumbed red

along the fore-edges like a thousand lips,
are gilded on heads and tails, the gilt half-faded.

Out of the biblical plagues of the 1930s,
black storms of dust, vast ravening clouds

of grasshoppers, comes this blasted, smoking heirloom,
a nut-brown flap of torn and weathered leather

wrapping a slab of paper. Its English
plunges into my heart like a small black bird.

Ex Patria

Some nights I stand before my bookcase,
touching the spines. The household gods
are murmuring in their sleep.

At last I take a volume,
open its paper cover
like a hatch, and my mind climbs down

to the half-remembered
country I have left:

the same ethereal smell of cold,
the same snow-light in the air
from the blue snow squeaking underfoot,

the same flakes falling in the silent road
among branches of the silver maple
where the scarlet cardinal shakes himself and sings.

I want to take it all in,
and I do—so far in, so strangely
and imperfectly inside me

it has to change itself to be there
because I've changed.
A fresh breeze rises

in the branches. The cardinal utters
something through his mask. It's too much.
I close the hatch.

A Weekend in Vienna

All the bookstore windows were festooned
with swastikas. (Hitler's secretary's
memoirs had just been published
in a new edition.) In the Ringstrasse,
a whole neighborhood of Imperial architecture—
brilliant center of the Austro-Hungarian Empire completed
just before the Imperial collapse. Roman ruins
below street level in Michaelerplatz,
and in the Kunsthistorisches Museum
the Habsburg treasure hoard: I stood
before Pieter Breughel's *Tower of Babel*
for half an hour. Reclining bronze Goethe
outside the Burggarten; the Neue Burg balcony where
Hitler harangued the Austrians; and in Judenplatz,
a small concrete bunker (Holocaust Memorial).
The banner hung from a nearby building bore
Andy Warhol's pop art Chairman Mao.

You took a picture of me, remember, outside
Freud's office. And we stood in the street under
Mozart's apartment window. Wiener schnitzel
in a pub near the university, coffee and cake
at the Sacher Hotel. In the English bookstore,
no sign of my coveted translation
of *The Man Without Qualities,* so I bought
a Thomas Bernhard novel instead, *Old Masters.*

We stood on the ramparts of Stephansdom.
You swam in the Danube, and back at the hotel
sobbed at our childlessness.

My one regret: we never stayed
at that discreet and elegant hotel—the Orient—
whose rooms were offered only by the hour.

And yet, in some concrete postwar pile
somewhere at the University of Vienna,
we stood before a doorless

and endlessly moving paternoster,
and, holding hands, stepped onto it together.

Amelia Island, Florida

July afternoon. The beach wide open
for miles in both directions. A few walkers,

a dog, one canted red beach umbrella
in the distance: in its shade, the only

human lying down out here is reading
a book. Two sandpipers browse the surf,

a seagull wobbles in the air, and behind us
in the wide, high dune, sea rockets, sea oats,

a wooden staircase back to the waiting car.
I stand behind a beach-wide line of shells,

bare feet in the sand and dressed for sun.
My wife plays in the surf, running

with our boy who's almost four years old.
(It's the first time he's met the ocean

in person.) She kneels in the wet sand, knees
apart, and each time the surf comes in

it swells the skirt of her summer dress with foam.
Our boy runs back and forth between us,

down to the water to tumble in the waves
and let his mother kiss him, then back up

to peer at me or throw his arms around
my legs before he's off across the sand

again to his mother. The Atlantic
here is the color of my parents' eyes,

slate blue. It's hot, the sun is dazzling,
the hypnotic rollers roaring as if a boy

were smoothly turning the volume up then
down on a snowy analog TV

which broadcasts the fourteen-billion-year-old news.

II

Sailing to Babylon

I sailed a boat to Babylon
and rowed back lonely in the rain.
I struck out down a country lane,
I set my course for Avalon,

but once I'd crossed the Acheron
and slept beside the silver Seine,
I sailed my boat to Babylon
and rowed back lonely in the rain.

I've worshipped at the Parthenon,
I've loved the girls of Aquitaine,
but when they lay my bones in Spain,
O tell the Tetragrammaton
I sailed my boat to Babylon
and rowed back lonely in the rain.

Prow

*Ship's figurehead, Provincial Roman or
Germanic, 4th-6th century A.D., in the
British Museum*

Raised above slashing whale-roads like a hand
gripping an oar of air, this oaken prow
once craned its latticed neck and thrust its whorled
and hook-beaked orb-head like a bird of prey

into the streaming hail. But plunges now
over those moving mounds of sea in dreams
alone, and only dreams that heavier mound,
black loam where king and silver slept their dooms

with arm-rings, weapons, cauldrons, armor, ship
that rowed toward Valhalla through the dark.
And sometimes it grows troubled in its sleep—
the sail's in rags above the heaving deck,

the crew pulls hard for open water, blind,
lashing the icy ropes against the wind.

Prague

Someone had left a mannequin in the street.
It was wearing a wedding dress
and—but no,

it was a woman, standing on a box.
A small crowd had gathered around her
and her eyes were closed.

I hesitated. Then
reached down to the jar at her feet
as if I were bending to pet a stranger's dog.

And as though I had deposited a soul, *chink,*
her eyelids fluttered open,
her fingers flickered,

she awoke like Hermione
astonishing her husband
in the miraculous final scene of *The Winter's Tale.*

Later, through the window of a restaurant,
I saw her dash across a crowded street,
clutching her skirts to keep them from the rain.

House

Its glassy look suggests one hypnotized
from gazing at the house across the street
as if into a mirror: a man half-crazed
with disappointed love. Look how distraught

after the vivid morning he appears
now in the gathering shade of afternoon,
how filled with darkness, how the darkness pours
like flames in silence out of every pane

across the unmowed lawn into the trees.
But when the stifling air grows vague with dusk,
and the sky is overwhelmed with cloudy towers
that blot the stars like battlements of dust,

the boy inside turns on the lights and sings
the sympathy of not inhuman things.

Mortgage

I've bought a house here it is inside me

it has plenty of windows a good roof
I built a lot of it myself

there are good schools nearby and parks
a fine bookstore as my agent said
location location location

the stairs are a little worn out
the basement leaks
small animals are living I think down there

the ghost in the attic he's more than interesting

I've been remodeling lately
adding some bedrooms a porch
it's so expensive

what's in it? hundreds of books
a piano a bed for dreaming

I invite people over for dinner we have long talks

I still haven't finished unpacking
I've got to hang some paintings on the walls

my friends who rent say
how do you make the payments you have to work so hard

I tell them without my house where would I live

The Museum of Death

In the Museum of Death the guests are eating lunch
made from a dead man's recipe.
They use knives and forks invented by the dead.

Everyone sits in a room
built by those who are no longer with us,
everyone speaking words the dead have made.

Everything is archaeological:
prayer, toilets, table manners, cash.
Even the air was once breathed by the dead.

Look how impatiently the curator taps
his fingers on his desk. It's getting late.
Very soon the guests will have to go.

III

Glenn Gould on the Telephone

Tel Aviv, 1958

Stockholm to Salzburg, and Berlin to Rome,
and so far I've had six good hotel rooms,
five comfortable beds—and at most three
adequate pianos. But today's
instrument was so hopelessly unwieldy
I decided it was best to just ignore it;
it required a kind of mystical
transcendence to get me through the night.
Of course it is a desert country,
as they keep explaining to me, and so they
have desert pianos, understandably
enough. But this damnable monstrosity,
whose maker shall remain unnamed, played me
instead of the other way around.
At this afternoon's rehearsal it finally
got to me. I was playing like a pig.
Out of sheer desperation I drove off
into the desert outside Tel Aviv
in a car I'd rented in Jerusalem
and parked among the giant dunes to think.
I just sat there alone and looked out
at that white expanse of desert and the sea
and thought of—well, in fact I imagined—
fields of snow, a frozen lake, a vast
hibernal landscape, gloomy, white and gray.

But imagined it, if you will, in the sense
of performing a spiritual exercise:
as seen through the window of the living room
at my cottage. I saw the chesterfield,
the coffee table and the leather chair,
the Tiffany lamp with the slightly tilted shade,
the phonograph in the corner, and before
me as I turned around in my chair,
my Chickering, now sixty-three years old,
beloved instrument of the stubby legs
and boxy-sided lyre. Here was that good,
immediate tactile grab, the true five-speed
manual transmission of pianos.
Here was that relationship of depth
of touch to aftertouch which seemed almost
a harpsichord's in its solicitude,
and gave me a strong sensation of control.
I felt, as I began to play, almost
as if my fingers were striking the strings
directly. The concerto gathered like
the gray oncoming clouds of a winter storm.

Then—what a shock to come back to myself
in the desert! But, clinging desperately
to my image of the Chickering, I
drove back to Tel Aviv and rushed backstage.
And you know how I get before I play
Beethoven, how I always have to wind
myself into a kind of silk cocoon.
I soaked my arms as usual, but in silence,

feeling I was back in Uptergrove
soaking in the bathroom sink, that I was
about to step into the living room
on a cloudy winter day and play alone.
I've no idea whether when I stepped
onto the stage I gave the audience
so much as a nod. As far as I was
concerned, I suppose, it wasn't really there.
I sat down. Then the orchestra began
to play; and yet I had the distinct feeling
it was playing only in my mind.
When my turn came I found at first I could
barely move the keys—I felt a jolt
of pure terror, as you can imagine,
which lasted for a few moments; but then
rhythmically the concerto settled down,
as I'd been unable to get it to
on that piano in rehearsal, and
soon I began actually to enjoy
the new sensation—one of distance, of
a physical removal from the keys.
Then time turned to glass. And it seemed I
heard the concerto with my inward ear,
which is to say I heard my inner self.

And yet something else happened afterward,
after the concert tonight, I mean, which
I'm also sure I never will forget.
A man and a woman came straight backstage
and introduced themselves. It was Max Brod,

Kafka's friend and, indeed, literary
executor, which was remarkable
enough. And then the woman—I believe
she was Brod's secretary—revealed to me
they had heard me play the same concerto
some nights ago, but that tonight I seemed
in an elevated frame of mind: "You
were not quite one of us. Your being was
removed." This was the finest compliment
I have ever received. Of course, I bowed
deeply, but then I only said, "Thank you,"
because, I confess, I was hesitant
to name the spirit that had passed between us.
For this was evidence, I felt, of
a spiritual communication which
must be possible between performer
and listener even in live performance.
True, it was only possible because
I had achieved an almost hermetic
state of isolation from my audience.
My soul, if you will, was elsewhere, alone.
And yet the fact remains that these no doubt
unusually perceptive people saw,
or heard, or knew I wasn't there. In fact
it's really much too spooky to explain.
As if I really was in Uptergrove—
this evening, I mean, while I was on the stage.
As if these people managed to perceive,
by listening to the music, I was gone.

Northrop Frye at Bowles Lunch

"I have had sudden visions."

Bloor Street, Toronto, 1934

3 a.m. in the all-night diner, dizzy
with Benzedrine and lack of sleep, old books

and papers scattered across the table.
With his pen, his Dickensian spectacles,

his *pounding, driving bourgeois intellect,*
he charges into a poem by William Blake

with two facts and a thesis, cuts *Milton*
open on the table like a murdered corpse

and *spins it like a teetotum* until
he's put each sentence through its purgatory

and made the poet bless him with a sign:
thus (though perhaps one can picture this

only from a point outside of time)
he sees the shattered universe around him

explode in reverse, and make the flying
shards of its blue rose window whole again.

Northwest Passage

Henry Hudson, his final voyage, 1610-11

If you should fail to find your passage north
across the Arctic Ocean to Cathay,

and fail again to find your northeast passage
above the frozen coast of Muscovy

beyond Nova Zembla and the Gulf of Ob,
then fail heartbreakingly in seeking westward

two hundred miles upriver at Norumbega
until your good ship almost runs aground;

and if you should rig again your old *Discovery*,
trimming your sails for your northwest way at last,

and cross the sea to Resolution Island,
that most fog-laden threshold in the world,

and drive into the Furious Overfall
foaming in the mouth of that forbidding strait

drawn on the map by those who sailed before you
that far only, threading your delicate way

through a labyrinth of ice-floes in the wind,
a nightmare of rain and cloud, fog and snow,

and mutiny kindling and covered in the cabins;
and if, steering by heaven and your compass,

you should name the towering landmarks as you go—
Desire Provoketh and, some leagues beyond,

Cape Hopes Advance, the island Holde with Hope;
yea, if a huge wind plow the booming ice

against you, till you set anchor for safety
far to the south in a vast but dead-end bay

and freeze there all that winter in the dark;
in your desperation, before you make a plan

in secret to explore some other way
and set out in the shallop in the spring,

leading your own personal mutiny
against yourself by leaving your command;

before you come back having failed again;
before the last rebellion of your starving crew

drives you back to the shallop with your son,
your mate, and five mariners, sick and lame,

and sails guilty and terrified back to England;
haul anchor, sailor, trim your sails for home,

and, before you raise Cape Hopes Advance,
name the breaking ice-field Patience Bay.

Map of the Interior

The explorer David Thompson (1770-1857)

I like to think how he prepared himself
for fifty thousand miles of traveling

on foot and by canoe by reading books.
A Grey Coat Schoolboy off Westminster Abbey.

Gulliver's Travels, Robinson Crusoe,
the Persian and Arabian Nights. (He says

in his book somewhere that *Hudson Bay is*
a place Sinbad the Sailor never saw,

as he makes no mention of Musketoes.)
I see him peering through his microscope

at the two-piece *Musketoe Bill* (whose upper shaft
is black, three-sided, sharp; the lower *a round*

white tube like clear glass; and the mouth inverted
upwards. For with the upper part the skin

is punctured, then the clear tube is inserted
in the wound.) I picture him in the Rockies on

some vast defile of snow, his frightened men
boring a hole to see how deep the drift

lies under them. They can't plumb the bottom;
but he notices that perfect wound glows blue—

light near the surface, deepening to navy—
and wonders at the immensity of water

raised from the Pacific to that height,
salt ocean to fresh snow, *mysterious*

circulations on a scale so vast
the human mind is lost in contemplation.

In what year was he the first to comprehend
that huge system of interior plains

from which the Nelson and Saskatchewan
and Mackenzie, with all their tributaries,

pour their heart's blood out into the sea
like three titanic arteries of a body

supine as a sleeping giant's body?
All night he would lie beneath the stars

with a case of instruments, observing moon,
planets, constellations, breaking his quills

to calculate positions for the streams
and mountains, hills and lakes, and set them down

in numbers for translation to his map.
But a map's nothing but an image of the world

made small enough to hold inside the mind,
as different from the wilderness itself

as an anatomical chart is from a man.
His art was science—he never pretended

otherwise—even if the *voyageurs*
and Natives thought he could raise the wind

and saw the future through his telescope
and knew the men there and saw what they were doing.

For what he really knew he learned from them:
to give careful attention to all things,

the smallest stone, the bent or broken twig,
learned it from Native hunters in the field

for whom all such things spoke plain language.
For that was how you found your way at last

out of the great black forest to the place
exactly where you always meant to go.

IV

Quarry Park

Madison, Wisconsin

I followed my son into the April wood—
a tall two-and-a-half-year-old and I
on my fortieth birthday. He understood

what we were there to see and do, and why,
and raced off down the path among the trees,
stopping when some fresh puzzle caught his eye:

a panicked ant, a white stone, working bees.
He'd turn aside and call out, "Daddy, look!"
and there was nothing I could do to please

my guide until I crouched down low and took
the ant, or worm, or stone into my gaze,
the way we'd peer together at a book,

and comment or exclaim. But still the day's
purpose lay ahead: to find The Mountain,
as he called it, somewhere inside that maze

of mountain-biking trails and vegetation,
and climb. Soon there it was, our afternoon's
steep, treed hill. And at once, because he can,

that boy scrambles up, the way raccoons
do, using hands and feet, more than half way,
then has to stop. You've seen how, in cartoons,

Coyote will face the camera in dismay,
hovering mid-air above the canyon?
(He knows too well the bird has got away.)

So with a silent blink of resignation
Felix twists his neck to glance at me;
then, without complaint or hesitation,

he slides on his belly down the muddy scree.
As a father will who likes to have his say
at such moments, I gently suggest he—

but no: he digs his fingers in the clay,
toes the jutting crags, grunts, hauls himself up
over and over, learning how to play

The Mountain like a new game, has to stop
again twice more at the same stage of his climb
to lie face down in the mud of a steep

smooth patch with no handholds, and grinds that grime
full frontal into his jeans and t-shirt
on the slide back down. And then, every time,

stands back up to attack the cliff of dirt.
His fourth attempt, he masters the smooth patch
by grasping a jutting tree root hacked curt

for landing mountain-bikes, and with dispatch
hoists himself the last few feet to the crest.
Then, like the victor in a wrestling match,

charged with his achievement, and its cost,
he throws his arms into the air and shouts,
"I did it!" Well. His father is impressed.

Let no one deny the boy's got guts.
I climb up a gentler slope and bend down
to high-five the little champion where he squats

already peering at some ants, a crown
or bough of leaves trembling above his ears.
Then I straighten up, sigh, and look around

at the green ranks of budding volunteers,
white ash trees with fuzzy clusters, and these
honey locusts whose green-yellow flowers

troll the air with pollen for the bees,
and the pendulous catkins of the paper birch,
the air aromatic with the sex of trees

and quiet as the transept of a church
on weekday afternoons. That's when I hear
a piercing melody blast from some high perch

in the branches above our heads: *cheer, cheer,*
calls the cardinal, in a voice who could forget:
purty, purty, purty. Out of sheer

joy, I whistle up my cardinal minuet—
and catch Felix looking up at me, as though,
or in fact, bemused by this sudden duet

of Daddy and birdie. He doesn't know
he's not the only boy who's ever bested
such a hill, or that thirty years ago,

alone in a wood that, for a while, existed,
I learned to whistle like a cardinal
by failing frequently, that I persisted

until I'd honed my imitational
fluting into a good loud cardinal song
true enough to make a real bird signal

back to me I hadn't got it wrong.
Or that I slogged those fogbound woods for hours
in rubber boots, poling myself along

fallen tree trunks with a stick whose powers
and nature changed to match my fantasy.
If past the leafless trees there rose the towers

of Castle Marvelous, then by alchemy
I was Percival with his magic spear.
But if to slow my advance the German army

had blown the dikes along the Dutch frontier
and swamped the Rhineland to the knees in mud,
then I was my uncle in a bandolier

humping my Bren gun through the Hochwald flood.
Always anywhere other than where I was:
Ontario woodlot. And yet I should

have imagined differently, I suppose,
if I had known the history of the place:
Brébeuf striding black-robed through the trees

with his *Grammaire,* his crucifix, and grace
into the Great Death; or Chief Child-of-the-Sun,
Tsouharissen, with his black tattoos,

driving his naked army of Chonnonton,
those Deer People with their flint-head arrows,
westward to assault the Mascouten.

Abruptly, while I'm conjuring ancient blows,
my reverie is arrested by the song
of our cardinal overhead. (Suppose

you don't realize the volume's on
and, by mistake, you open an audio file—
forgetting, since you've had them on so long,

you're wearing earphones—and suddenly high style
gorgeous music breaks out between your ears;
that's how that cardinal sounds.) My son's smile

shines straight up to where the bird appears
perched on a branch of the budding linden tree
that crowns the hill, a shock of red feathers

in the pale-green downy leaves. We can see
him open and close his scarlet beak and ripple
his shoulders and black throat with such esprit

his long tail feathers bob, though his more supple
crest stays steady, and the music pours
like changes from a bell-tower whose steeple

draws a bright world around it where it soars.
He's making himself at home, or rather,
making a home for himself among the stars,

building a territory out of blather.
I think I can imagine how he feels.
He stops to listen and look for some other

red-feathered bird who'd like to take his meals
in this vicinity, then takes a breath
and fires off another round of peals

into the clearing and the teeth of death:
What cheer. What cheer. Wait, wait, wait, wait, wait, wait.
His practiced challenge hurtles down the path

we took to get here, and flies out to meet
our future selves on the path we'll take to leave.
It blows into the bushes where his mate

moves urgently, I imagine, to weave
grass, weed stems, dead leaves, soft bark ribbons
into a wood's-edge nest, a cup for love,

to hold a clutch of eggs. I guess she's got plans.
She's counting on him to make that music good.
Their fledglings, once their singing school begins,

will have the finest teacher in the wood.
Some day their songs may break into the hearts
of mountain-bikers and be understood

by solitary walkers, teach the arts
of dogged perseverance to old dads
with their dogs and children, light-heeled upstarts

with God knows what wild visions in their heads,
boys who will return without their parents
to play in the tree-forts built by bygone kids,

their branches stacked in conical monuments
like tangled pickup sticks or naked tipis
whose brown bark roofs and tree-limb battlements

under the slanting trunks of fallen trees
lie hidden in the leafy underbrush.
The songs of our bold cardinal's young trainees

will with all their variations gush
from an ancient spring of cardinal melody
that filled the air here when this stand of bush

was just a spare stone quarry in the country
a hundred years ago. Or maybe not.
I seem to recall their cardinal ancestry

edged up from southeastward to this spot
in the Midwest just fifty years ago
or thereabouts: immigrants, I'd forgot,

like me. And Felix; who now wants to go,
he says, having lost interest in our cardinal.
He takes a narrow path through this plateau

we're on, leading me down a diagonal
singletrack, as the bikers call it, and
over a gamut of recreational

obstacles and terrain, our one-bird band
and I resuming our call-and-response
duet, showing off our sure command

of ostinato variation, once
in a while even whistling in unison
across the space between us, and we advance

over muddy trails and many a root system,
the trees sticking their feet out to trip us,
I say, though my son has to learn the lesson

falling to his hands and knees; nevertheless,
on through gullies and kettles and over ridges
strewn with glacial rubble we digress,

down drops and over jumps and makeshift bridges
and natural half-pipes of this beehive network,
plunging through underbrush and clouds of midges,

choosing our random way at every fork
until we emerge into another clearing
and stumble on a focus of the park,

a campfire pit filled with ash and kindling
charred on one end, and bits of broken glass,
the remains of someone's bonfire doused hissing

in mid-roar. By the garbage in the grass
it appears the party ended months ago,
likely last fall. There are few sights more crass

than such wreckage bared by the melted snow,
crumpled beer cans and smoked cigarettes
and plastic hot dog wrappers—ugly, though

certainly not as ugly as it gets;
and yet it looks like they had a good time.
I warn my son against dabbling in the pit's

alluring glitter and intriguing grime,
though all the while that most erotic joy
of teenage bonfire parties, the sublime

drunkenness and theolepsy of a boy
charged with sexual jealousy and ardor,
fills my memory. Once I was the toy

of deities in the blood, and someone's daughter,
killing me just to know how it feels
to be so bad. In such a theater

as this, what the midsummer night reveals
is strong gods striving in the human chest,
and overhead a blur of stars that wheels

slowly around the heavy earth possessed
by nothing but gigantic solitude.
While my boy sits down on a log to rest

and poke the ashes with a stick, and brood,
I peer into the well of sky overhead
encircled by the trees, my thoughts subdued

by our cardinal's falling mute—his having said
all he means to say, at least for now—
and imagine the changing weather which, instead

of this cobalt, or besides it, sends new
messages day and night to Quarry Park:
sun, moon, stars, rain, low thunderheads, pale blue

winter dawns, loud blizzards in the dark,
lightning, gray Brutalist concrete overcast
days-on-end, white cumulus, autumn's stark

windstorms, noctilucent clouds, the vast
calm of a sunny summer afternoon,
crepuscular rays, contrails, the black massed

invasion of a looming roll cloud, strewn
confetti of golden leaves, and falling snow,
and ricocheting hailstones, opportune

dewfalls of an August morning, and slow
fogs drifting up among the trees.
Now Felix is saying he wants to go

home to see Mommy, asking if I'll please
carry him on my shoulders. Yes, I will.
I lift him over my head, feel him squeeze

my neck with his thighs, and set off downhill
toward where we came in, grasping his ankles
in my hands. I suppose if life can fill

this strange park full of history and fables
for this loved boy, he'll be at home here.
Once Huge Toad—as old Huron chronicles

of this ancient world call the latest glacier—
laid this excavated drumlin we're exploring
like an egg half-buried in the lithosphere,

with all our city's drumlins, a long string
of oblong eggs in parallel formation,
and loaded it with rubble, commingling

sand, clay, silt, and gravel by the ton
with many erratic cobblestones and boulders,
like this pink granitic gneiss, and this collection

of schist or slate sticking half out in spurs
from the muddy trail around my feet.
I set Felix down to show him the colors

of quartz pebbles and sandstone in a sweet
armored mudstone till ball poking out
of the slope in front of us—then take a seat

on it to tie my shoelace. With a shout—
"Daddy! Come look!"—Felix, who has gone
ahead over the ridge we're on to scout

out the next gully, calls me to attention
and over the hill to see what he's found there.
"Cereal," he exclaims, and points one

middle finger at a trailside pair
of limestone blocks tattooed with fossils not
unlike his favorite breakfast, spilling their

mossy calcite circlets like a lot
of nuts and washers across a table. To me
they're either the holdfasts or scattershot

stalk plates of ancient feather-stars or sea
lilies, hundred-million-year-old runes
from when all this, as far as the eye can see,

was shallow ocean billowed by the moon's
long-distance lugging. My boy's tired. I swing
him yawning up into the afternoon's

brindled sunlight on my shoulders, turning
my thoughts, as I walk, to stone-age invention:
how ancient people lived here by hunting

mastodon and mammoth to extinction
with spears tipped in dark blue Moline chert
and silicified sandstone the colors of the sun

cut long and thin and shaped like works of art.
How later peoples who camped here in the forest
near the lake which with his melting heart

Huge Toad had left behind still did their best
with herds of elk and caribou and deer.
How when the centuries warmed the people fished

and hunted goose, muskrat, turtle, beaver;
and gathered acorns, wild rice, raspberries, roots;
and thought up the stone ax, spear thrower,

quern stone, pottery, awl; cremation, arts,
rituals, ossuaries; and long-distance trade
in blue-gray Indiana hornstone cherts,

Atlantic Ocean seashell, bright knife-blade
copper from Lake Superior, and rings,
axes, hooks, harpoons, and spear points made

by hammering hot copper till it sings;
and black volcanic glass from Yellowstone.
They understood the insistence of things

buried with the bodies of the lone
dead, that sad, beautiful meanings belong
to them not because of what they are alone,

but because of where they are, and whose; what song
the makers sang in making them, and why;
when they were made; from what; and how strong

the spirit was that taught the maker's eye
and guided the maker's hand to hammer, twist,
and polish the godsend metal. One may die

and three or four thousand years later consist
of one ordinary skeleton and a few
things whose meanings an archaeologist

can for all her care only construe:
for instance, the ground-up iron ore
the Red Ocher people employed here to

decorate or cover as if with gore
the corpses of the dead; though we can guess
it means the blood of ritual rebirth or,

simply, life, painted on as if to bless
the dead one with another. It's because
they had no writing that they could impress

each thing with only part of what it was.
But here the rocky path begins to curve
sharply downward to the right, just as

I realize I'm going to have to swerve
my passenger carefully around a low-
hanging leafy ash tree bough alive

with fuzzy purple clusters, so I slow
down and tell Felix to duck his head—
but he stops me with a shouted "No!"

grasping the tree-limb with his hand instead,
and nearly pulling himself off my shoulders
in the process. At his command I spread

the leaves apart, uncovering what appears
to be, and is, a little flock of pale-
green, grazing aphids, guarded by their herders:

perhaps a dozen black ants, big and hale
from their diet of aphid nectar. We see
one now, inconspicuous on this scale,

who milks an aphid with her antennae
by stroking its abdomen, and then drinks
the secreted bead of clear liquid slowly

as a connoisseur. But soon their near flank's
assaulted by a sudden ladybug
landing with her elytra askew; the ranks

race in from all directions and plug
the gap with soldiers (this being just enough
to keep all but one green charge safe) and tug

that red-and-black tank of a predator off
the branch still crushing a frantic aphid
in its jaws. I'm unnerved to hear my son laugh

at this, but I remember he's a kid,
and let the branch go, and make him duck
as we pass underneath, leaving the vivid

death behind us. Still, this weird attack
keeps happening in my memory as we go
down the shady path again. I'm struck

that such killing is going on below
our feet, above our heads, and everywhere,
even in our own bodies, even now.

What a hell this garden is. I'm aware
even so that without killing there would be
no evolution, nothing human. Nature

makes beauty into death abundantly
and death into beauty; though if they'd never
started farming aphids on some tree

thirty million years ago, those clever
ants would still be a strange modest class
of tropical wingless wasps forever

scavenging or hunting prey en masse
in cloudy jungles—and not as pervasive
an ecological champion as grass.

So with ancient men. It's easy to believe
that, once some woman had the ingenious thought,
they planted gardens here; and, unless grave

drought killed all the seedlings in the plot,
ate sunflower seeds, squash, and later corn
and beans; and this changed them—they were not

nomads now but villagers, and were born
and lived and died in the same places not far
from here on the lakeshores, and came to mourn

and bury their dead in great circular
mounds on high savannah drumlins such
as this. Later they built short linear

mounds close to those round ones, and then much
longer ones on hillsides pointing down
to lakeshores, springs, and wetlands, and then such

enormous effigies of birds to crown
a hilltop, and bears feet-down on the slopes,
and water spirits that seemed to have grown

tails longer than giant telescopes
with their heads pointing downstream, geese and snakes
and flocks of thunderbirds, and whole landscapes

of thousands of figures among the lakes,
rivers, hills, and limestone caves of this region,
its wide rolling grasslands and scattered oaks

under the revolutions of the sun.
Five hundred years of this, then it stopped for good;
invading war made them abandon

everything.—A breakneck flash of red
in the air above fractures my thought
for a moment, until I've understood

our cardinal's back; he reaches out to light
on a locust branch beside the trail
ahead and holds on, balancing his weight

on the bouncing tree limb with his tail
and making no sound except a flittering
of wings. Though it occurs to me to hail

him with a whistle and make him sing,
something tells me no; instead I ask
Felix in a whisper if he saw him swing

out of the air into the tree and frisk
his ruffled feathers with his claw. When we
approach he turns his obsidian eye and mask

to watch us, then flits to another tree
a little further down the path and waits
for us to catch up to him, apparently,

only to take off again in spates
of fluttering. I think there must be some
reason for the funny game this invites,

and I get the uncanny if welcome
feeling that our cardinal intends
to take us somewhere like a meddlesome

spirit in a story. Then he ascends
suddenly out of sight and is gone forever.
I stop walking. I was thinking of the mounds,

spirits, thunderbirds: that men took over
this land by massacre, that settlers came
amazed by what they found here and, however,

began plowing once they'd staked their claim,
erasing the sacred landscape mound
by mound. Still, some sites do remain;

some were rebuilt; and sometimes when they found
a site, some archaeologists noted
where it was and even surveyed the ground

and drew a map. This drumlin is depicted
as a mound site on one large-scale chart
I've seen published—though no map was completed

of the site itself before it became just
a quarry. And now, gradually, I find
with all our wandering off we've gotten lost;

so I lower Felix gently to the ground
and look around us. At once a humming bee
wavers into view and leads my boy spellbound

off the trail and into a little sea
of hyacinths and a grove of mountain ash.
When I was a boy we called this the Wizard Tree

because its berries, which we liked to mash
gorily between finger and thumb,
had five-pointed stars. Which was balderdash

to my father the forester, so we kept mum.
He called them rowan trees. I happen to know
that a boy and his mother once planted them

all over the place here sixty years ago,
or sixty-five; that's what the neighbors say.
Apparently they've used the time to grow.

When summer comes they'll pour a milky way
of flowers down the park and come August
each branch will offer up a red array

of berries to the birds. Although they've just
started to bud, somehow I recognize
them by their pale smooth bark: the prettiest

trees in all these woods to my late eyes
that remember how they'll look in other seasons.
The Celts, who have been known to fetishize

their trees, employed the rowan for protections
of all kinds, and chiefly magical.
My father would have called them superstitions

but I like knowing the supernatural
histories of things: that magic wands
and staffs and crosses once were made (and still

are in certain enclaves) from the rowans.
That they were trees of the Goddess, Faerie wood.
And that their berry's pentagram corresponds—

so ancient paganism understood—
to the four elements supervised by spirit;
which is to say the world. As for that good

boy who planted these trees here and thus lit
our park with radiant flowers and bright lanterns
of berry clusters every summer that

ripen from green to red—my neighbor explains
he was the old quarry-keeper's son,
James. He was the kind of kid who learns

how to read and once he has begun
prefers it even to running in the woods
and playing baseball in the air and sun,

although he liked those too, and liked his friends.
James lived in a four-room shack somewhere deep
in the woods, with an outhouse, enough beds

down below and in the attic to sleep
eight children and their parents, one wood stove,
a root cellar out back in which to keep

milk and other perishables, a trove
of flashlights and kerosene lamps for light,
a big rain barrel for wash water (save

for winter when they melted snow), and sweet
drinking water from the neighbors—since all
around them, down below, street by street,

the city's affluent West Side, its mall,
university, and hospitals, spread out
over the farmland, practicing its sprawl.

Still, here they stayed, living on, half-caught
in the nineteenth century, caring for
these seventeen lofty acres without

so much as a title to the land or
a lock on the door, mowing, trimming boughs,
and planting flowers long after the poor

quarry went defunct. I watch Felix browse
the family's grove of naked rowan trees—
the Corcorans' grove. But no sign of their house

remains: the house where, upstairs, James would seize
the night, reading in bed by kerosene
lamp or old flashlight, augmenting these

with a little mirror on the wall, keen
on comic books and *Treasure Island,*
Robin Hood and Huckleberry Finn,

stretched out with a paperback in hand,
the beagle curled at his feet, and his head
in Camelot or Never Never Land.

One day when he was twelve his mother said,
"Jim, we're going out to plant some rowans
in the yard around the house," and led

him outside with a couple of tin cans
full of seeds. Two of his older brothers
and a sister—not long after Japan's

attack on the Pacific Fleet—their mother's
protests notwithstanding, had joined the war;
and I suspect the rowan's magic powers

of protection in ancient Irish lore
rose in the heart of Mrs. Corcoran
that morning. And one can hardly ignore

their name is a Gaelic word meaning "crimson,"
just as "rowan" is Proto-Germanic
for "getting red"; to a medieval Christian

the pentagram on the berry got its magic
by standing for the five red wounds of Christ,
and was thus proof against the witch's trick

and fiend's temptation; should you be enticed
by the Devil himself, it was the berries'
color that might forestall your getting diced-

for in the gambling rooms of Hell, for cherries
are not so red as rowan berries. James
watched the rowans grow until the city's

illicit Elysium flowered here. The games
of the Corcoran children and their friends
thinned out as they grew up, the righteous claims

of death and war and marriage put hard ends
to household memberships, and before long
James was the kind of lonely man who spends

his old age frittering away among
the wreckage of his childhood and the flowers
his mother planted in the yard. Along

the muddy paths the miniature towers
of purple crocuses have broken through,
and because we're walking here they're ours;

these hyacinth clusters in white and blue,
these yellow trumpet-flower daffodils,
these snowdrops with their drooping heads, this slew

of purple glory-of-the-snow that spills
down the hillside all along the trail
Felix and I are taking—it all fills

me with such longing, for God knows how frail
our lives and their monuments are, and yet
how beautiful the ruins that prevail

even in the midst of death; how we forget,
and how our forgetting makes us homeless,
until we dig ourselves out of this debt

we owe the giant past for making us
ourselves. Felix smells a way out at last,
and leads me toward a flowery egress

which I can see we're now approaching fast
by the glimpse of sky as we descend,
though I slow down to watch him struggle past

a stair of roots that threatens to upend
him at any moment. He knows this maze
at least as well as I do; it's his friend

if not his home already, and the days
of his tree-climbing and mountain-biking
youth ride out before him in a blaze

of summer afternoons; he'll be the king
of Quarry Park before he's twelve, God
willing, and may he love each lovely thing

the more, as he grows into his manhood,
for knowing its history; I'd have him feel
he can make a home out of any good,

livable place on Earth, if it be real,
by learning where he is. He's stumbling down
the last few muddy steps to where he'll

fall into the road and break his crown
if I'm not careful, so I run ahead
and catch him by the jacket, and we're blown

by our momentum crashing through a bed
of crocuses, thrown nearly off our feet
backwards until we find ourselves instead

cast out into sunshine in the street.

Notes

The first two sentences of "Glenn Gould on the Telephone" are adapted from the film *32 Short Films About Glenn Gould* (1993), directed by François Girard. A few other passages in the poem are adapted from published interviews with Gould, collected in *Conversations with Glenn Gould,* by Jonathan Cott.

The first epigraph to "Northrop Frye at Bowles Lunch" is taken from an interview with Frye, which may be found in *Northrop Frye in Conversation,* edited by David Cayley. The passages in italics (except for the title of Blake's poem, *Milton*) are quoted or adapted from Frye's letters in *The Correspondence of Northrop Frye and Helen Kemp, 1932-1939,* edited by Robert Denham.

In "Map of the Interior," the passages in italics (aside from one French word and some book titles) are quotations from David Thompson's book of travels. For a scholarly edition, see *The Writings of David Thompson, Volume 1: The Travels, 1850 Version,* edited with an introduction by William E. Moreau.

JAMES POLLOCK grew up in southern Ontario, Canada. He graduated summa cum laude with an Honors B.A. in English literature and creative writing from York University in Toronto, and earned an M.A. and Ph.D. in creative writing and literature from the University of Houston, where he held several fellowships in poetry. He was a John Woods Scholar in poetry at the Prague Summer Program at Charles University in Prague, and a work-study scholar in poetry at the Bread Loaf Writers' Conference. His poems have been published in *AGNI, The Paris Review, Poetry Daily,* and more than a dozen other journals. His critical reviews have appeared in *Contemporary Poetry Review, Books in Canada, The New Quarterly,* and elsewhere, and a collection of his criticism, *You Are Here: Essays on the Art of Poetry in Canada,* is forthcoming from The Porcupine's Quill. He is an Associate Professor at Loras College in Dubuque, Iowa, where he teaches poetry in the creative writing program. He lives in Madison, Wisconsin.